Nahj Al-Balaghah
(Peak of Eloquence)
for Children

Published by

Tahrike Tarsile Qur'an, Inc.

Publishers & Distributors of the Holy Qur'an
80-08 51st Avenue
Elmhurst, New York 11373

Published by

Tahrike Tarsile Qur'an, Inc.

Publishers & Distributors of the Holy Qur'an

80-08 51st Avenue

Elmhurst, New York 11373

http://www.koranusa.org

E-mail: read@koranusa.org

Edited by

Bilqis Esmail, Noreen Jafri & Leigh Marucchi

First U.S. Edition 2006

Library of Congress Catalog Number: 2003100900

British Library Cataloguing in Publication Data

ISBN: 1-879402-08-4

Courtesy of:

Ahl Al-Bayt World Assembly

Typing & Typesetting by Bilqis Esmail

paintingsart@yahoo.com

Foreword

Hazrat Ali was a uniquely superb personality. He was a multi-faceted and multi-directional divine entity. At a time he was a poet, a philosopher, a warrior, a jurist, a mystic, a leader and an orator. Such people are rarely found in the treasure of nature. Nahjul Balagha is a book consisting of his sermons, letters and speeches compiled by Seyyed Razi in the fifth century. According to historical record these sermons and letters were collected by different people at different times. We find a portion of this material in the books of Sheikh Saddooq, Sheikh Mufid and Sheikh Toosi and many others. The sermons of Hazrat Ali are full of spiritual, social and political sagacity. It is really a compendium of wisdom. It teaches us about the philosophy of monotheism. What are the secrets and latent mysteries of God. We learn about God and his creatures - Nahjul Balagha is a marvelous literary and intellectual treatise. After the Qur'an no book can excel it in beauty of idiom, style and thought.

In the present book, we are presenting some lines of Hazrat Ali from Nahjul Balagha for the interest of children. They are about birds, sky, stars, rivers, fountains, herbs, peacocks and so many other natural objects. We want our children to know much about the life and universe in the light of Nahjul Balagha. We hope our effort will be appreciated.

Prof. Maqsood Jafri
April 2004

Introduction

Nahj Al Balaghah for Children is a collection of small portion of speeches given by Ali ibn Abu Talib (pbuh).

Ali ibn Abu Talib (pbuh) was the only person ever to have born inside the Kabaa, on 13th Rajab, about 610 A.D. He was the cousin and son-in-law of Prophet Muhammad (pbuhahh), the trustee of the Prophet, a champion of the early battles and man of great wisdom and patience.

These passages are taken from a larger collection, the Nahj Al Balaghah, (Peak of Eloquence) which contains his speeches, sermons, letters and sayings. The sermons contain philosophy of monotheism, lectures on character building, piety, truth and justice, and tributes to Prophet Muhammad. The original collection is a masterpiece of Arabic prose and is next only to the Quran in its beauty which is difficult to translate, especially for children.

Note:
Allah is an Arabic word meaning God, the same God of Abraham, Moses and Jesus.
Pbuh is an abbreviation for 'peace be upon him'.
Pbuhahh is an abbreviation for 'peace be upon him and his family'.

Mrs. Noreen Jafri
New Jersey, U.S.A.

The creation

Allah made creation without an example to follow and without help or advice from anyone. The heavens and the earth include mankind and all other creatures and millions of stars. Man is himself but a tiny part of creation. And God Who created the whole of the Worlds is able to do much more wonderful things than can enter the imagination of man. He originates creation, and repeats it, without any flaws. None can create like Him. Praise be to Allah!

Sermon 154

The earth

He created the earth. He hung it in space without any legs or pillars to hold it up.

We provide sustenance of every kind, physical, mental, spiritual, etc. for mankind. Every kind of thing is produced on the earth in due balance and measure. The mineral kingdom supports the vegetable, and they in their turn support the animal, and there is a link of mutual dependance between them.

Sermon 185

The winds

He made the winds blow with his kindness. The winds convert the dead land into a living, fertile, and beautiful land bearing a rich harvest. Not only does the wind cool and purirify the air, and bring the blessings of rain, it also helps international trade and interaction among people through sea-ways and now, by air-ways.

Sermon 1

The moon

Then he decorated the sky with stars, meteors, a shinning sun and glowing moon each in an orbit to travel

Sermon 1

The night

Praise to Allah when night falls and darkens, and praise to Allah when stars rise and set.
The darkness of the night is as a covering. Just as a covering protects us from exposure to cold or heat, so this covering gives us spiritual respite from the buffets of the material world, and from the tiring activities of our own inner exertions to sleep and rest.
Both the Night and the Day have each its own beauty and its utility for man. Night is a period of darkness. When the night spreads her veil, the sun's light is hidden, but not lost.

Sermon 48

The sun

Look at the sun and
moon,
plants and trees, water
and stones. Look at the
change of day and night,
the gush of oceans, the
height of mountain peaks
and the variety of
languages we speak.

Sermon 184

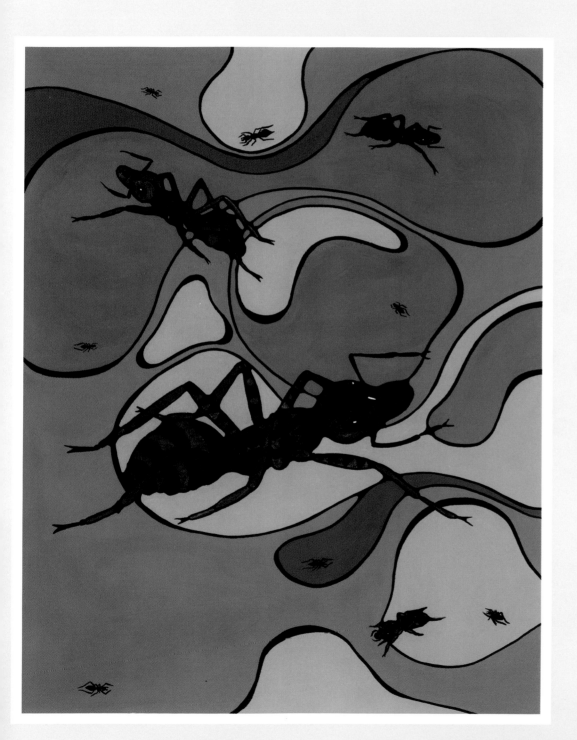

The ant

Look at the ant, small and
delicate. See how it
crawls in search of food.
It carries grain to its hole
and stores it in summer
(in its tunnel), to use in
winter.
It collects for its
time of weakness
while it is strong.

Sermon 184

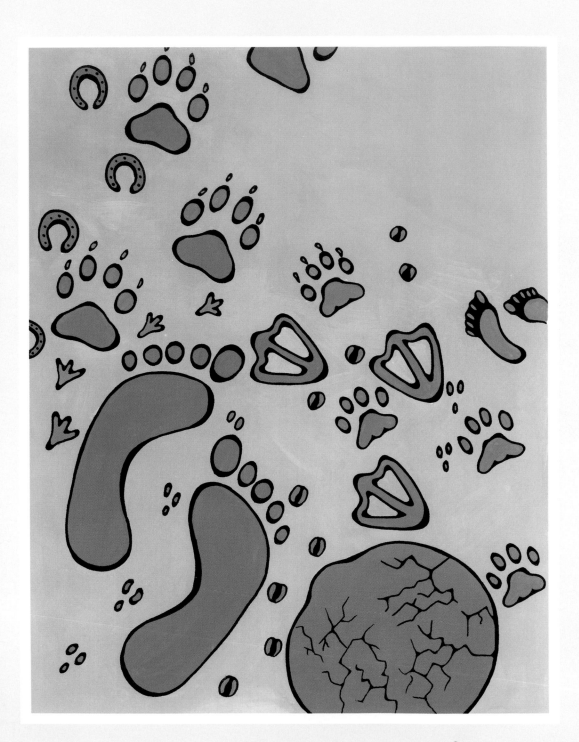

The feet

Glory to Allah, He
gave feet
to the ant and the
gnat, and created
animals bigger than
them, like fish and
elephant.

Sermon 165

The locust

I will tell you about the
locust. Allah gave it
two red eyes,
with pupils like moons.
He gave it small ears,
mouth and sharp
senses. He gave it
two front teeth to cut
with and feet that grip.

Sermon 185

The birds

Birds obey Allah's commands. He knows how many feathers they have and how many breaths they take. He made their feet able to stand on water and land. The flight of birds is one of the most beautiful and wonderful things in nature. The make and arrangement of their feathers and bones, and their stream-line shapes, from beak to tail are instances of purposive adaptation. They soar with outstretched wings; they dart about with folded wings; their motions upwards and downwards, as well as their stabilisation in the air, and when they rest on their feet, have given many ideas to man in the science and art of aeronautics. But who taught or gave to birds this wonderful adaptation? None, but Allah, Whose infinite Mercy provides for every creature just those conditions which are best adapted for its life.

Sermon 185

10

The peacock

The most amazing bird is the peacock. Allah arranged its colors delightfully. He layered its feathers to form wings and gave it a long tail.

Sermon164

The bat

A marvel of His creation is the bat. It hides from daylight even though daylight brings other creatures into action.
And, it is active at night, even though most other creatures stop their activities that time.

Sermon 154

The fish

Allah is aware
of the cries
of beast in forests, the
sins of people in
private, the
movement of fish,
and stirring of water
by strong winds.

Sermon197

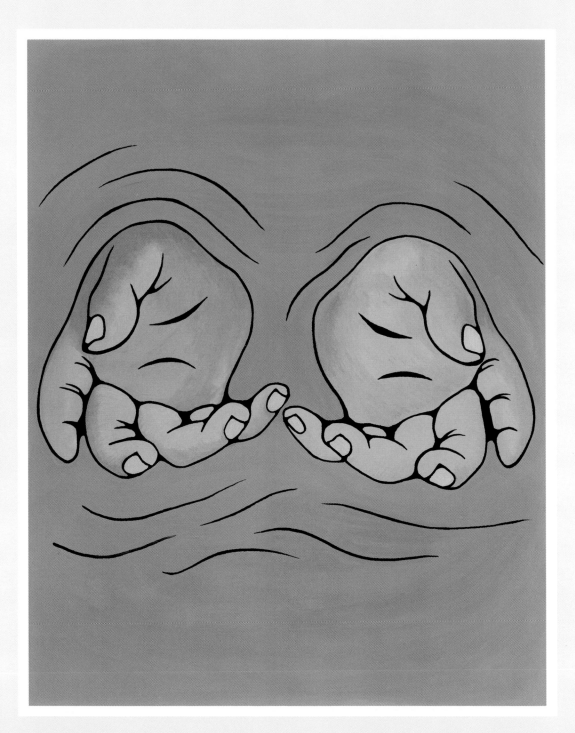

Livelihood

All creation obeys
Him and all creation
exists because of Him.
He is the hope of all
the poor, the honor of
the humiliated, the
might of the weak, the
comfort of those who
are sad. He hears
what every speaker
says and knows secret
thoughts of those who
keep silent. He gives
livelihood to
every living thing, and
everything returns to
Him when it dies.

Sermon108

David

The Psalms was revealed to David (peace be upon him). He used to make baskets from palm leaves with his own hands. He would ask his companions, " Which of you will help me by buying one?" With the money he earned, he would buy barley bread.

David was a man of exceptional strength. He was mocked by his enemies, and even by his own elder brother. But he relied upon God, and won through and afterwards became the king. He was a good and just king.

Sermon 159

Herbs

Moses (peace be upon him) said, " My Lord, I need whatever good you send me." He asked Allah for bread because he only had herbs for food. His skin was so thin that the green color of herbs could be seen through his belly!

Glory be to Allah has created everything in pairs - in man, in animal life, in vegetable life and possibily in other things of which we have no knowledge..

Sermon 159

The winter

I will tell you about Jesus, (peace be upon him) son of Mary. He had a stone for his pillow, wore coarse clothes and ate rough food. At night the moon was his lamp and in winter the earth was his shade. His feet were his transport and his hands were his servants.

Sermon 160

Good tidings

Then Allah sent Muhammad (pbuhahh) as a witness, a carrier of good news and a warner. As a child he was the best in the universe, and as a grown up he was the purest, the best in behavior and the most generous.

Sermon105

The people of Arabia

Allah sent Muhammad (pbuhahh) as a warner to all the worlds and trusted him to receive His revelation. While you, the people of Arabia followed the worst religion; lived among harsh rocks, poisonous snakes, drank muddy water, ate filthy food, and killed each other.

Sermon 26

Idols

Allah sent Muhammad (pbuhahh) with truth to turn His people away from worshipping idols and towards worshipping Him (Allah): away from obeying Satan and towards obeying Him.

Sermon 145

The Prophet

Every people or generation or nation had its Message or Messenger : God revealed Himself to it in some way or another. Different gifts and different modes of procedure are prescribed to God's Apostles in different ages, and perhaps their degrees are different though it is not for us mortals with our imperfect knowledge, to make any difference between one and another of God's Apostles. The Apostles were sent to preach and teach - to preach hope to the repentant ("good news"), and to warn the rebellious of the Wrath to come.

Your Prophet is the best and purest. He is the role model to follow. Allah loves those who follow His Prophet's example. He would sit on the ground when eating; he would sit like a slave. He mended his shoes with his own hands and patched his clothes himself.

Sermon 160

The revelation

When the Holy Quran was revealed to the Prophet I (Ali) heard a wailing cry. I (Ali) said, " O Messenger of Allah, what is this wailing?" He replied, " That is Satan, who has lost all hope of being worshipped. O Ali you see what I see and hear what I hear, only you are not a prophet; you are a vicegerent and on the path of virtues."

Sermon 191

The stars

The example of the household of Muhammad (pbuhahh) is like the stars of heaven; when one sets another rises.

Sermon 99

The rain

The riser has risen, the sparkler has sparkled, and the appearer has appeared. Allah has replaced one group of people with another. We waited for these changes just like those suffering from famine wait for rain. The Imams are vicegerents of Allah over His creatures. They make Allah known to people. No one will enter Paradise without knowing the Imam.

Sermon 151

The Holy Quran

The Qur'an is a final revelation, revealed to Prophet Muhammad. It was revealed after the Torah and Bible. It is a book of wisdom which makes things clear, and it teaches you to love, share, forgive, etc. It is a marvellous book, and even a single verse cannot be produced by any person, other than Allah. It contains guidelines for mankind to carry on their day to day activities, and a universal message for all, which is why it attracts people of all faiths.

Sermon 17

The leader

Those in the Prophet's household have the best human virtues described in the Quran. They are the treasure of Allah. When they speak, they speak the truth, and when they are quiet, no one can outshine them. A leader should speak truthfully to his people, and should use all his intelligence. He should be one of those who work for the next world, because he has come from there and will return there.

Sermon 59

The tree of Prophethood

We are the tree of Prophethood, the place where Revelation descended, the place where angels visited, the main spring of knowledge. Those who help us and love us shall have (Allah's) mercy. Those who hate us shall have (Allah's) punishment.

Sermon 108

A lamp in darkness

A leader is like a lamp in darkness. Anyone walking in the dark has to take light from it.

Sermon 186

A grain of barley

If I were given the seven heavens and all they contain in exchange for disobeying Allah, by taking the husk of a grain of barley from an ant- I would not do it.

Sermon 224

Two loaves of bread

Praise is due to Allah, from Whose Mercy no one loses hope, from Whose bounty no one is deprived, from Whose forgiveness no one is disappointed and for Whose worship no one is too high. His mercy never ceases, and His bounty is never missed.

You should know that out of the comforts of the world, your Imam (Imam Ali pbuh) had two torn pieces of clothing and two loaves of bread for his meal.

Sermon 45

The mosquito

Even if all living beings,
birds and beasts all come
together to try to create a
mosquito, they
will never be able to do it.

Sermon 186

Paradise

Today is the day
of preparation
and tomorrow and is
the day of contest.
The finishing point is
Paradise and those
who fail to reach it
will land in hell fire.

The final destination of
the righteous is the
Paradise, and it is a
promise of Allah. It is a
garden, with rivers
flowing.

Sermon 28

The earth's produce

Allah makes His creatures bear hardship when they do evil deeds, by reducing the earth's produce, holding back blessings and blocking benefits, so that those who wish to ask for forgiveness may ask.

Sermon 142

Water

You should know that every action is like the fruit of a tree. A tree needs water. A tree that gets good water is healthy and its fruit is sweet. A tree that grows on bad water is unhealthy and its fruit is bitter.

Sermon 153

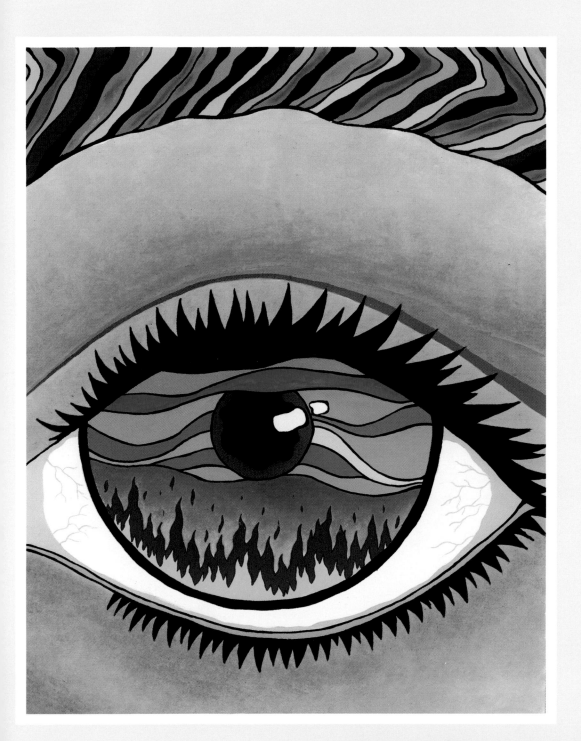

With insight

The person who sees with
his heart and acts with
insight, thinks before
doing anything.
If the action is good for
him, he does it, but if it is
harmful he does not.

Sermon 153

Off the path

The person who acts without knowledge is like someone who walks off the path, when he is off the path he gets farther away from where he was going. But the person who acts with knowledge is like someone who walks on the clear path.
So you should see if you are moving towards your goal or are getting farther away from it.

Sermon 153

The spring of hearts

Learn the Quran because
it is the most wonderful
speech and the
spring of hearts. Heal
yourselves with its light
because it is a cure for
sick hearts.
Recite it in the best
manner because it is the
fairest of accounts.

Sermon 109

Prayer

And be regular in prayer, and regular in charity: And whatever good you send forth for your souls before you (from this life), you shall find it with Allah: Surely, Allah sees well all that you do. And say: "O my Lord! You grant forgiveness and mercy! Because You are the Best of those who show mercy Pledge yourselves to prayer and pay special attention to it. Pray as much as you can and try to get closer to Allah by it.

Sermon 198

The sacred house

The Kaabah, the house of Allah was built by Prophet Abraham, and his son, Ismail. Allah requires you to make Hajj (pilgrimage) to His sacred house, atleast once in your lifetime, which is the qiblah for mankind. This is a place full of peace and tranquility.

The first House (of worship) appointed for men was Kaabah, full of blessing, and of guidance for all beings. Whoever enters it attains security. Pilgrimage to it is a duty that men owe to Allah, those who can afford the journey; but if anyone denies faith, Allah does not need help from any of His creatures.

Sermon 1

Jihad (Struggle)

The most difficult Jihad is with one's self, to do what is right and to avoid what is wrong. Jihad is one of the gateways of Paradise that Allah opened for His special friends.

Those who believe, and work hard with their strength, in Allah's cause, with their wealth and their person, hold the highest position in the Sight of Allah: They are the people who will achieve salvation.

Sermon 27

The Strongest

Remember, trees that grow in the desert have the strongest fibers, while luscious green trees have soft wood. Desert bushes make good fuel and their fire is slow in dying out.

And, when you are strong, do not oppress the weak.

Letter 45

Life

O Allah, send down Your mercy; send down Your rain for us. Send an amount that will be good for us, satisfy our thirst and make the land green with grass. So that all that has withered will grow again and all that has died return to life. A rain which produces plenty of fruits, watering the plains, flooding the valleys, giving leaves to trees, and bring prices down. Surely You are able to do whatever You will.

Sermon 142

INDEX OF
NAHJ AL-BALAGHA